*"There are a thousand questions
which cannot be answered. It is hypocritical
to state that human freedom and the absolute freedom
of the market are inseparable concepts, as if laws of this
kind, which have emerged from the most selfish, unequal
and merciless systems ever known, were compatible with
freedom for human beings, who the system has turned
into mere commodities. It would be much more exact
to say that without equality and fraternity, which
were the sacrosanct watchwords of the bourgeois
revolution, there can never be liberty,
and that equality and fraternity are
absolutely incompatible with the
laws of the market."*

The

Gigantic

Casino

Fidel Castro

The Gigantic Casino

REFLECTIONS ON THE WORLD FINANCIAL CRISIS

LeftWord

First published in February 2009 by
LeftWord Books
12 Rajendra Prasad Road
New Delhi 110001
INDIA
www.leftword.com

LeftWord Books is a division of
Naya Rasta Publishers Pvt. Ltd.

ISBN 978-81-87496-82-3

Printed at
Repro Knowledgecast Limited, Thane

Contents

Speech on the 40th Anniversary of the Cuban Revolution

JANUARY 1, 1999

People of Santiago: Compatriots in all of Cuba:

I am trying to recall that night of January 1, 1959; I am reliving and perceiving impressions and details as if everything were occurring at this very moment. It seems unreal that destiny has given us the rare privilege of once more speaking to the people of Santiago de Cuba from this very same place, 40 years later.

Before dawn on that day, with the arrival of the news that the dictator and the main figures of his opprobrious regime had fled in the face of the irrepressible advance of our forces, for a few seconds I felt a strange sensation of emptiness. How was that incredible victory possible in just over 24 months, starting from that moment on December 18, 1956, when — after the extremely severe setback which virtually annihilated our detachment — we managed to gather together seven rifles to resume the battle against a combination of military forces which totaled 800,000 armed men, thousands of trained officers, high morale, attractive privileges, a totally unquestioned myth of invincibility, infallible advising and guaranteed supplies from the United States? Just ideas which a valiant people claimed as their own worked a military and political victory. Subsequent vain and ridiculous attempts to salvage what remained of that exploiting and oppressive system were swept away by the Rebel Army, the workers and the rest of the people in 24 hours.

Our fleeting sadness at the moment of victory was nostalgia for the experiences we had lived through, the vivid memory of the comrades who fell throughout the struggle, a full awareness that those exceptionally difficult and adverse years obliged us to be better than we were, and to transform them into the most fruitful and creative ones of our lives. We had to abandon our mountains, our rural life, our habits of absolute and obligatory austerity, our tense life of constant vigilance in the face of an enemy that could appear by land or air at any moment of the 761 days of the war; a healthy, hard, pure life and one of great sacrifices and shared dangers, in which men become brothers and their best virtues flourish, together with the infinite capacity for commitment, selflessness and altruism that all humans carry within them.

The enormous difference in equipment and strength between the enemy and us forced us to do the impossible. Suffice it to say that we won the war with rifles and anti-tank mines, in every important action always fighting against the enemy's artillery, armored vehicles and, in particular, airplanes, which were always immediately present in any military action.

We seized rifles and other semi-automatic and automatic light infantry weapons from the enemy in combat, and the explosives with which, in rustic workshops, we manufactured the shells we used against armoured vehicles and their accompanying infantry always came from the rain of bombs which they launched against us, some of which failed to explode. The infallible tactic of attacking the enemy when it was on the move was a key factor. The art of provoking those forces into moving out of their well-fortified and generally invulnerable positions became one of our commands' greatest skills.

Enemy operations units and their garrisons were besieged, their reinforcements were destroyed or they were forced to surrender out of hunger and thirst, under constant fire from our marksmen, who tightened their circle every day avoiding frontal attacks, which cost many lives when adequate equipment and weapons are unavailable. What we learned in the mountains and dense forest areas was applied there in the lowland areas, on paved highways, under cover of citrus plantations, fruit orchards and even cane fields, which served to conceal our troops, generally rookies, given the accelerated growth of our ranks as arms were acquired, although always under the command of more experienced comrades, mounting surprise attacks on reinforcements. The same method wound up being applied within the cities, isolating the garrison's various positions.

That was how the city of Palma Soriano was taken in just three days, and that was how the plan was conceived to attack and take control of the garrison of 5,000 men in the Santiago de Cuba plaza, with the deployment of 1,200 rebel troops. Previously, 100 of the weapons taken in Palma had been brought in through Santiago Bay to start the uprising, five days before the start of operations where the four battalions defending the periphery gradually moved in to encircle the city. I am omitting more precise details of the plan conceived. I will simply note that there was one rebel fighter for every four enemy soldiers. We had never had a more favourable balance of forces.

The battle was initiated in Guisa, a few kilometers from Bayamo, by 180 men, who were to fight against reinforcements sent on a paved highway and other routes from that city, where the enemy army and thousands of its best soldiers were located, with backup from heavy tanks. After 11 days of intensive combat, in which our forces were growing with the arms taken and some small reinforcements, Guisa fell into our hands on November 30, 1958.

This battle was yet another example of the exceptional fighting capacity acquired by our soldiers and of their swift action. Five months previously, in June of the same year, the enemy had launched its last and apparently unbeatable offensive against the general command in La Plata, in the Sierra Maestra. But we were no longer the greenhorns who disembarked on December 2, 1956. Neither were we so numerous. The defence was initiated with approximately 170 men, with the combined and still very limited number of troops commanded by Che, Camilo, Ramiro and Almeida, who had received instructions to move towards Column No. 1's positions, the strategic objective of the enemy offensive. Thus, we had all our columns except the 2nd Eastern Front commanded by Raúl, which was too far away in the northeastern mountains to support our front. Four weeks later, we totaled around 300 fighters. Furthermore, hundreds of young unarmed volunteers were training in the Minas del Frío recruitment school.

CAMILO AND CHE'S MARCH FROM
THE SIERRA TO THE ESCAMBRAY

After 74 days of intense fighting, the enemy battalions had
suffered close to 1,000 casualties, including deaths,
wounded and prisoners. We were holding over 440
prisoners and we handed them back a few days later
through the International Red Cross. I have written what I
remember. Perhaps historians can be more precise
concerning this data, based on our documents, which have
been preserved, and those that were later discovered in
enemy archives. What I can confirm is that over 500
weapons were captured and as they were seized from the
army they were used to arm the trainees. Without wasting
any time, when the fighting was over, the rebel columns,
comprising no more than 900 armed men, moved into the
territory dominated by the army towards the centre of the
country, with the exception of the extensive eastern zone
already under the firm control of the Frank País 2nd
Eastern Front. Those rebel columns advanced in different
directions, creating new war fronts that were rapidly
developed. I remained in the command post with a few
men. While carrying out those operations, Che and Camilo,
the first with approximately 140 men — according to my
recollection, without consulting any records — and the
second, with around 100, carried out one of the greatest
feats among the many I know from history books: they
advanced more than 400 kilometers from the Sierra
Maestra to the Escambray mountain range — in the wake
of a hurricane — through low-lying swampy areas,
infested with mosquitoes and enemy troops, under constant

aerial vigilance, without guides, without food, and without the logistical support of our underground movement, which had a weak organization in the area of their long march. Outwitting sieges, ambushes, successive lines of contention and bombardments, they reached their goal. Such was our confidence in the fighters who routed the enemy offensive and, most important of all, such was their infinite confidence in themselves and their legendary leaders. They were men of iron. I recommend that young people read and reread the beautiful descriptions contained in Che's *Pasajes de la guerra revolucionaria (Episodes of the Revolutionary War)*.

And as I have almost involuntarily fallen into these reflections of our battles in the Sierra Maestra, to complete the history of the events which led me once again to this beautiful city on that January 1st whose 40th anniversary we are celebrating today, I will tell you that I left La Plata with 30 armed men and 1,000 unarmed recruits on November 11. Those valiant and selfless young men had more experience with hunger, bombardments and a lack of everything than they did with arms, given that there wasn't even a spare bullet for real shooting practice. They arrived in enthusiastic waves at the school, from all over, but at that time only one out of every 10 was able to endure those conditions. They nourished our ranks, they were more daring than our older fighters. Inspired by the traditions and stories they heard, they wanted to achieve in one day what others had done over several years.

Collecting small rebel units along the march, plus the weapons from two enemy detachments that came over into our ranks, persuaded by then Commander Quevedo, our worthy and valiant adversary in the battle of Jigüe, and on the understanding that they would not fight against their former comrades in arms, our large column constituted an advance guard of 180 men with weapons of war. In Guisa, Baire, Jiguaní, Maffo and Palma Soriano, scenes of numerous actions, and with the support of other forces as we advanced, the recruits more than realized their dreams of fighting. Partially taking into account losses through the death, injury or illness of already-equipped fighters, and with the arms seized with the taking of Palma, which I estimate at around 700 all together, all the recruits that left La Plata with me six weeks earlier were armed and constituted a formidable force. In Palma alone, 350 weapons were taken.

I should point out that not all the arms that contributed to converting the youth at our Minas del Frío school into front-line soldiers were exclusively the fruit of our triumphs. In mid-December we received what in my judgment constituted the most valuable arms aid from abroad: 150 semiautomatic weapons and a FAL automatic for me, dispatched in the name of the Venezuelan people by Rear Admiral Larrazábal and the revolutionary junta which had assumed power in Venezuela some months before the Cuban triumph. As you can imagine, those arms rapidly went into action and participated in the Jiguaní, Maffo and Palma Soriano combats.

For that reason, after Palma and Maffo fell under our control, there were more than sufficient weapons for our unarmed fighters, and we were able to send the aforementioned 100 troops for the Santiago uprising and a significant number to Belarmino Castilla, with instructions to cut off the retreat of the battalion located in Mayarí.

Since I mentioned the Venezuelan aid, I should state that in our revolutionary struggle we didn't receive arms and ammunition supplies from abroad, except in very exceptional cases, of which, out of the rest I recall or heard about, the Venezuelan consignment was by far the largest. Over 90 per cent of the arms and ammunition with which we armed ourselves and won the war were seized from the enemy in combat. They only amounted to a few thousand but, on an inviolate principle, absolutely all of them were always used on the front line. The events that I have recalled only partially have been commemorated throughout the year that has just ended.

Honour and eternal glory, infinite respect and affection to those that died then to make possible the country's definitive independence; for all those who wrote that epic in the mountains, the plains and cities; to the underground guerrillas and fighters; to those who, after the triumph, died in other glorious missions or loyally gave up their youth and energies to the cause of justice, sovereignty and the redemption of their people; to those who have died and to those who are still living; because, if that January 1 could be spoken of as the triumph attained in five years, five months and five days starting on July 26, 1953, on this anniversary — taking the same starting point — it is accurate to speak of a heroic and admirable struggle of 45 years, five months and five days.

FOR THE YOUNGEST GENERATIONS
THE REVOLUTION HAS BARELY BEGUN

Even today, the Revolution has barely begun for the youngest generations. A day like this would have no meaning if I do not speak for them.

Who are those who are present here? In their overwhelming majority they are not the same men, women and young people of that time. The people I am addressing are not the people of that January 1. They are not the same men and women. It is another, distinct people and, at the same time, the same eternal people.

Of the 11,142,700 inhabitants that constitute the country's current population, 7,190,400 had not yet been born; 1,359,698 were under 10 years of age; the overwhelming majority of those then aged 50 and who would now be at least 90 have died, even though those living beyond that age are constantly more numerous.

Of those compatriots, 30 per cent were unable to read and write; I believe that a further 60 per cent never reached sixth grade. Only a few dozen technical colleges and high schools existed, not all of them within the reach of the people; the same with teacher training colleges, plus three universities and one private one. Professors and teachers amounted to 22,000. Possibly 5 per cent of adults, that is, 250,000 persons, could have had more than a sixth-grade education.

There are some statistics I remember.

Today, much better trained teachers and working professors total over 250,000; doctors, 64,000; university graduates, 600,000. Illiteracy has been eradicated, it's extremely rare to find a person who hasn't reached sixth grade. Education is obligatory up to ninth grade; without exception, everyone who reaches that level can continue high-school level studies free of charge. There's no need to refer to absolutely accurate and absolutely exact data. There are facts that no one would dare to deny. Today, with pride, we are the country with the highest per capita indices of teachers, doctors and physical education and sports instructors in the world; and we have the lowest infant and maternal mortality rates in the Third World.

Nonetheless, I don't propose to talk of these and our many other social achievements. There are far more important things than these. What is an absolute reality is that there is no possible comparison between today's people and yesterday's people.

Yesterday's people, illiterate and semi-illiterate, and with really only a minimal political awareness, were capable of making the Revolution, of defending the nation, of subsequently achieving an exceptional political consciousness and initiating a revolutionary process that is unparalleled in this hemisphere and in the world. I do not say that out of any ridiculous chauvinistic spirit, or with the absurd pretension of believing ourselves better than others; I am saying it because, as a result of fate or destiny, the Revolution that was born on that January 1 has been subjected to the hardest trial faced by any revolutionary process in the world.

With the participation of three generations, our heroic people of yesterday and today, our eternal people, have resisted 40 years of aggression, blockade, and economic, political and ideological warfare waged by the strongest and richest imperialist power that has ever existed in the history of the world. The most extraordinary page of glory, and of patriotic and revolutionary determination has been written during these years of the special period, when we were left absolutely alone in the middle of the West, 90 miles from the United States, and we decided to carry on.

NO CAUSE IS MORE IMPORTANT THAN
THE CAUSE OF HUMANITY ITSELF

Our people aren't any better than other peoples. Their historic greatness is derived from the singular fact of having been put to the test and having been able to withstand it. It's not a great people in and of itself, but rather a people, which has made itself great, and its capacity to do so is born out of the greatness of the ideas and the righteousness of the causes it defends. There are no other causes like these, and there have never been. Today it's not a matter of selfishly defending a national cause; in today's world an exclusively national cause cannot be a great cause in and of itself; our world, as a consequence of its own development and historical evolution, is globalizing quickly, unhaltingly and irreversibly. Without abandoning national and cultural identities and even the legitimate interests of the peoples of each country, no cause is more important than global cause, that is, the cause of humanity itself.

Nor is it our fault or our merit that for the people of today and tomorrow, the struggle begun on January 1, 1959, has inexorably turned into a struggle along with other peoples for the interests of all humanity. No country on its own, no matter how big or rich — not to mention a medium-sized or small country — can solve its problems on its own. Only those with limited vision, those who are politically shortsighted or blind, or who are completely devoid of concern and sensitivity toward human destiny, could deny that reality.

But the solutions for humanity will not come from the goodwill of those who rule and exploit the world, even though they can't conceive of anything except what constitutes heaven for them and hell for the rest of humanity, a real and inescapable hell.

The economic order, which dominates the planet, will inevitably fall. Even a child in school who knows how to add, subtract, multiply and divide well enough to pass an arithmetic test can understand that.

Many take recourse in the infantile practice of calling those who talk about these subjects skeptics. There are even those who dream of establishing colonies on the moon or Mars. I don't blame them for dreaming. Maybe if they achieve that, it will be the place where some can take refuge, if the brutal and growing aggression against our planet is not halted.

The current system is unsustainable because it is based on blind and chaotic laws which are ruinous and destructive to society and nature.

The very theoreticians of neoliberal globalization, that system's best academics, spokespersons and defenders are unsure, hesitant, contradictory. There are a thousand questions which cannot be answered. It is hypocritical to state that human freedom and the absolute freedom of the market are inseparable concepts, as if laws of this kind, which have emerged from the most selfish, unequal and merciless systems ever known, were compatible with freedom for human beings, who the system has turned into mere commodities.

It would be much more exact to say that without equality and fraternity, which were the sacrosanct watchwords of the bourgeois revolution, there can never be liberty, and that equality and fraternity are absolutely incompatible with the laws of the market.

The tens of millions of children in the world who are forced to work, to prostitute themselves, to supply organs, to sell drugs in order to survive; the hundreds of millions of unemployed, critical poverty, the trafficking of drugs, of immigrants, of human organs, like the colonialism of the past and its dramatic legacy of underdevelopment today, and all of the social calamities in the world today, have arisen from systems based on these laws. It is impossible to forget that the struggle for markets led to the horrific butchery of the two world wars of this century.

We cannot ignore the fact that the principles of the market are an inseparable part of the historic development of humanity, but any rational person would have every right to reject the presumed perpetuation of such social principles as the foundation for the subsequent development of the human species. The most fanatical defenders of and believers in the market have converted it into a new religion. This is how the theology of the market emerged. Its academics, more than scientists, are theologians; for them, it is a question of faith. Out of respect for the genuine religions practiced honestly by billions of people throughout the world and out of respect for genuine theologians, we could simply add that the theology of the market is sectarian, fundamentalist and not ecumenical.

For many other reasons, the current world order is unsustainable. A biotechnologist would say that its genetic map contains numerous genes that lead to its own destruction.

New and unsuspected phenomena are emerging, ones which escape the control of governments and international financial institutions. It is no longer merely a matter of the artificial creation of fabulous wealth with no relation to the real economy. Such is the case of the hundreds of new multimillionaires who have emerged over recent years through the growth in the price of shares on the U.S. stock markets, like a giant balloon that inflates to absurd proportions with the serious risk that it will explode sooner or later. That is what happened in 1929, setting off a deep depression which lasted a decade.

In August of last year, the simple financial crisis in Russia, which produces only 2 per cent of the world's gross domestic product, caused the Dow Jones industrial average, which is the New York stock market's top indicator, to drop 512 points in one day. Panic set in, threatened to cause a crisis like that of Southeast Asia in Latin America and thereby seriously threatened the U.S. economy. They have barely been able to hold off disaster until now. The stocks traded on these stock exchanges include the savings and pension funds of 50 per cent of U.S. citizens. At the time of the 1929 crisis, those figures were only 5 per cent, and there were numerous suicides.

In a globalized world, what happens in any one place

has immediate repercussions on the rest of the planet. The recent scare was considerable. The resources of the world's wealthiest countries, summoned together by the United States, were mobilized to head off or attenuate the disaster. Nevertheless, they want to maintain Russia on the brink of the abyss, and are demanding unnecessarily tough conditions from Brazil. The International Monetary Fund has not moved a millimeter from its fundamentalist principles. The World Bank has rebelled and denounced the situation.

Everyone is talking about an international financial crisis; the only ones who haven't caught on are the citizens of the United States. They are spending more than ever, and their savings are less than zero. They're not concerned that their transnationals invest other people's money. Nor does it matter that the trade deficit continues to grow and has now reached 240 billion. They enjoy the privileges of the empire that prints the currency of the world's reserves. The speculators seek refuge in their treasury bonds *en masse* when there is a crisis. Because the domestic market is large and more money is being spent, the economy appears to be in good shape, although the profits of the corporations have decreased. Megamergers, euphoria; stock prices rise once again. They've gone back to playing Russian roulette. Everything will continue to go well eternally. The system's theoreticians have discovered the philosopher's stone. All points of access are intercepted to keep out the ghosts that could destroy the dream. It is no longer impossible to square the circle. There will never be a crisis.

But is the balloon that continues inflating the only

threat and the only speculative gamble? Another phenomenon that is reaching ever more fabulous and uncontrollable proportions is that of speculative operations involving currencies. These operations now represent a minimum of a trillion dollars a day. Some claim it to be 1.5 trillion. Scarcely 14 years ago, this figure was only 150 billion dollars a year. There could be confusion regarding the figures. It is difficult to express them, and even more so to translate them from English to Spanish. What we call a billion in Spanish, that is, a million million, is a trillion in North American English. On the other hand, a billion in North American English is a thousand million in Spanish. Now they have come up with the milliard, which means a thousand million in both Spanish and English. These language difficulties demonstrate how difficult it is to follow and comprehend the fabulous figures that reflect the degree of speculation in the current world economic order. The immense majority of the world's nations pay for it with the perennial risk of ruin. The slightest carelessness can lead the speculators to attack, devaluating the currency in any one of these nations, and liquidating their hard currency reserves, built up over decades perhaps, in a matter of days. The world order has created the conditions for this. Absolutely no one is or can be safe. The wolves, grouped in packs and aided by computer programs, know where to attack, when to attack and who to attack.

THERE ARE WORDS THAT CANNOT BE PRONOUNCED
IN THE TEMPLE OF THE FANATICS OF THE IMPOSED WORLD ORDER

Fourteen years ago, when this speculation was 2,000 times less, a Nobel laureate in economics proposed a 1 per cent tax on every speculative operation of this kind. Today the total that would have been generated through this 1 per cent would be sufficient to develop all of the countries of the Third World. It would be a way of regulating and holding back this harmful speculation. But, regulate? This would clash with the purest fundamentalist doctrine. There are words that cannot be pronounced in the temple of the fanatics of the imposed world order. For example: regulation, public enterprise, economic development programme, any minimal form of state planning, influence or participation in the economic area. All of this disturbs the idyllic dream of the free market and private enterprise paradise. Everything should be deregulated, even the labour market. Unemployment benefits should be reduced to the bare minimum, so as not to support "bums" and "freeloaders." The pension system should be restructured and privatized. The state should only concern itself with the police and the army, to maintain order, repress protest and wage war. It is not even permissible for it to participate in any way in the monetary policies of the central bank; this must be absolutely independent. Louis XIV would truly suffer, because if he said, "I am the state," today he would have to add, "I am absolutely nothing."

Apart from the frightful speculation with currencies, there has been an accelerated and unbelievable growth in so-called hedge funds and the derivatives market, another rather new term. I won't try to explain it. It's complicated. It would take a lot of time. I'll simply say that it is an additional system of speculative gambling, another enormous casino where the players bet anything and everything, based on sophisticated risk calculations generated by computers, high-level programmers and economic experts. They exploit insecurity and use the money in the banks' savings accounts. They have practically no restrictions, make huge profits and can provoke disasters.

The fact that the current economic order is unsustainable is evidenced by the very vulnerability and weakness of the system, which has turned the planet into a gigantic casino, and turned millions of citizens and sometimes even entire societies into gamblers, adulterating the function of money and of investments, given that they pursue neither the production nor the growth of the world's wealth, but rather a means to make money with money. Such a deformation will inevitably lead the world economy towards disaster.

A recent incident, which took place in the United States, has been the source of scandal and profound concern. One of the hedge funds that I mentioned and tried to explain in essence, precisely the most famous one in the United States, Long Term Capital Management, which has two Nobel laureates in economics and some of the best computer programmers in the world, and annual profits of over 30 per cent, was on the verge of bankruptcy, which would have had, it would seem, incalculable consequences.

Backed by the prestige it had acquired and depending blindly in the infallibility of its famed programmers and

Nobel Prize winners in economics, with a fund of only 4.5 million dollars, it mobilized funds from 75 different banks, totaling 120 billion dollars, for its speculative operations; that is, it obtained over 25 dollars in savings for every dollar of its own funds. That procedure broke all the parameters and supposed financial practices. The calculations and the programs failed. The losses were considerable; and bankruptcy — which is a dramatic word in this sphere — was inevitable. It was just a matter of days. The U.S. Federal Reserve System went to the rescue of the hedge fund, contradicting all the tenets of the United States and neoliberal philosophy, given that this was considered irresponsible behaviour on the part of that kind of institution. According to established principles, the hedge fund had to go bankrupt, the law of the market would teach it a lesson by imposing the relevant corrective. A scandal broke out. The Senate summoned Greenspan, the chairman of the Federal Reserve Board; he was called on to make a statement. This senior official, who came from Wall Street, is seen as one of the most expert and eminent figures in the U.S. economy. The principal merit for the current administration's economic success is attributed to him and he is currently enjoying special praise in financial and press circles as the man who halted the stock market crisis in the United States, by lowering interest rates three times in succession. After the president, he is viewed as the most important person in the country. Well, this famous and esteemed chairman of the Federal Reserve System informed the Senate that, if the hedge fund wasn't saved, it would lead to an economic catastrophe which would affect the United States and the entire world.

Where is the solidity of an economic order in which the action, qualified as adventurous and irresponsible, of a speculative institution which possessed a mere 4.5 billion dollars could lead the United States and the world to an economic disaster?

When a weakness and an immunological failure of such magnitude is perceived within the system, it could be diagnosed as suffering from something very similar to AIDS.

I don't wish to put forward any more arguments. Many other problems exist within the world economy. The prevailing order flip-flops between inflation, recession, deflation, potential overproduction crises, and sustained slumps of basic products. Countries as immensely rich as Saudi Arabia now have budget and trade deficits, even through every day they export eight million barrels of oil. Optimistic growth forecasts are evaporating. No one has the slightest idea of how to solve the problems of the Third World. What capital goods, technology, distribution networks, export credits do they have to seek markets, compete and export? Where are the consumers of their products? How are the resources to be found for health care in Africa, where 22 million HIV-positive persons would require, at current prices, 200 billion dollars every year to control one sole disease? How many will die before a protective vaccine or a medicine is found to eliminate the disease?

HOPEFULLY SOLUTIONS WON'T BE FOUND
AS A RESULT OF ECONOMIC CRISES

The world needs some leadership to confront its current realities. There are already six billion inhabitants on the planet. It is virtually certain that in just 50 years' time there will be 9.5 billion. Guaranteeing food, health care, education, employment, clothing, footwear, homes, drinking water, electricity and transportation for such an extraordinary number of persons who will be living precisely in the poorest countries will be a colossal challenge. First, consumption standards will have to be defined. We cannot continue introducing the tastes and ways of life inspired by the industrialized societies' wasteful model, which would be suicidal in addition to being impossible. The world's development must be programmed. That task cannot remain in the hands of the transnationals and left up to the blind and chaotic laws of the market. The United Nations is a good basis for this task, since it has a lot of information and experience; we must strive to make it more democratic, to put an end to the Security Council's dictatorship, and the dictatorship within the Council itself, or at least to increase the number of its permanent members so that the Third World is properly represented, with all the prerogatives enjoyed by the current members and changing the rules on decision making. Furthermore, the functions and authority of the General Assembly must be broadened.

Hopefully solutions won't be found as a result of economic crises. Billions of people in the Third World would be affected. An elemental awareness of the technological realities and the destructive power of modern weapons obliges us to think about the duty to prevent the inevitable conflicts of interest from leading to bloody wars.

The existence of a single superpower, of a global and asphyxiating economic order, makes it difficult — perhaps impossible — for even a revolution such as ours to survive, if it had been born today instead of when if could count on a source of support, in a world which was then bipolar. Because of that support, our country had the necessary time to develop an invincible capacity for resistance and to make known, in the international arena, the strong influence of its example and heroism, in order to carry out a great battle of ideas in all forums.

Peoples will keep on struggling, the masses will play an important and decisive role in those struggles, which in essence will be their response to the poverty and suffering to which they have been subjected, and thousands of creative and ingenious forms of pressure and political action will emerge. Economic crises and the absence of solutions within the established international economic system will destabilize many governments.

We are living though a stage in which events move more quickly than consciousness of the realities under which we suffer. We must sow ideas and unmask deceit, sophism and hypocrisy, using methods and means, which counteract the disinformation and institutionalized lies. The experience of 40 years of slander falling upon Cuba like torrential rain has taught us to trust the people's instincts and intelligence.

The European countries have given the world a good example of what can be achieved through the use of reason and intelligence. After centuries of internecine wars, they understood that even though they were wealthy industrialized countries, they couldn't survive isolated from one another. Soros, a well-known personality in the world of finance, and his group, in a speculative assault, brought Britain to its knees, despite the fact that Britain was once the head of a great empire, the undisputed queen of finances and the former ruler of the world's reserve currency, a role now played by the dollar and the United States.

The franc, peseta and lira also suffered the damage wrought by speculation. The dollar and the euro are keeping watch over one another. The dollar now faces a prospective adversary. The United States is anxiously wagering that the new currency will struggle and fail. We are keeping a close eye on events.

Anguish, uncertainty and doubt lead some to seek out eclectic alternatives. The world, nevertheless, has no other alternative to neoliberal globalization, which is dehumanizing, morally and socially indefensible, and ecologically and economically unsustainable, than a fair distribution of the riches that human beings are capable of creating with their dedicated labour and fertile intelligence. May there be an end to the tyranny of an order that imposes blind, anarchic and chaotic principles, that is leading the human species towards the abyss. May nature be saved. May national identities be preserved, and the cultures of all nations protected. May equality, fraternity, and with them, true liberty, prevail. The unfathomable differences between the rich and poor within each country and between countries cannot continue growing. They must, on the contrary, progressively diminish until they disappear someday. May merit, capacity, creative spirit, and what each individual actually contributes to the welfare of humanity, as opposed to theft, speculation, and the exploitation of the weakest determine differences. May humanism be genuinely practiced, with concrete actions and not hypocritical slogans.

TODAY'S STRUGGLE IS TOUGH AND DIFFICULT

Dear compatriots:

The nation that is waging the heroic battle of the special period to save the homeland, the Revolution and the conquests of socialism is advancing irrepressibly towards its goals, in the same way that the fighters led by Camilo and Che advanced from the Sierra Maestra to the Escambray. As Mella said, the future must always be better. Let's confirm this with the goals we have set ourselves for 1999. Let's consolidate and strengthen, work, struggle and fight with the spirit with which our heroic compatriots fought in Uvero, in the glorious days of the major enemy offensive, in the battles and the events we have recalled today. We have left behind the setback in Alegría de Pío, we have passed through Cinco Palmas, we have gathered forces, and now we are capable of triumph, just as 300 triumphed over 10,000; we are now much stronger, and certain of victory.

To all of our compatriots, and especially the young, I assure you that the next 40 years will be decisive for the world. Before you there are tasks that are incomparably more complex and difficult. New glorious goals await you;

the honour of being Cuban revolutionaries demands it. We will struggle for our nation and for humanity. And our voice can reach and will reach very far away.

Today's struggle is tough and difficult. In the ideological war, as in armed battles, there are also casualties. Not everyone has the courage to withstand these tough times and difficult conditions.

I was recalling today that in the midst of the war, in the midst of the bombings and countless deprivations, of all the young volunteers who entered the school, one in ten was able to withstand it; but that one was worth ten, a hundred, a thousand. By strengthening awareness, forming character, educating the young in the difficult school of life in our era, sowing solid ideas, using arguments that are irrefutable, preaching through example and trusting in the honour of humankind, we can ensure that for every ten, nine remain in their battle posts alongside the flag, the Revolution and the homeland.

Socialism or death! Patria o muerte Venceremos!

The Financial Ike

SEPTEMBER 18, 2008

There is no waste in today's afternoon news:

"Bush cancelled all his activities. He intended to travel to Alabama and Florida to participate in electoral fundraisers."

"He said on Thursday that he was worried about the financial markets and the US economy . . ."

"Markets have plummeted," cables continue to read, "the government was forced to nationalize the giant insurance company American International Group (AIG); and the Federal Reserve, in a coordinated action with other central banks, have injected 180 billion dollars into the financial markets.

"The President reaffirmed that his government is taking aggressive and extraordinary measures 'to appease the markets'.

"Authorities all over Asia are seeking to stop the devaluation of their currencies, stock exchanges and securities, to avoid the Wall Street crisis to affect the region.

"President of Brazil, Luiz Inácio Lula da Silva blamed today the international financial crisis on speculation, and admitted he was worried about a possible risk of a recession in the United States.

"He also felt sorry about the situation facing the big banks in the United States, which in the past criticized

Brazil and other emerging countries, and questioned the international financial system.

"'There is a crisis in the United States, a very strong crisis that has caused extraordinary unrest in the biggest economy of the world,' he said.

"'It is not that we are not worried. The United States is the world's biggest economy and major importer.'

"He concluded by saying: 'I see with certain sadness that important banks, very important banks, which had spent their whole life giving advice about Brazil and about what we should or should not do, are now bankrupt or have entered into bankruptcy.'"

The hurricane winds of the financial Ike are also threatening all "provinces" of the world. The weather forecast is uncertain; people have been speaking about it for weeks now, and gusts of more than 200 kilometres per hour are already being felt.

As Rubiera would say, its devastating power squares from one category into the next.

It is very difficult to closely follow and understand the very high figures of fresh money injected into the world's economy. Those are huge volumes of paper money leading inevitably to a decline in its value and purchasing power.

The increase in prices is inevitable in consumption societies and also disastrous for the emerging countries, as was pointed out by Lula da Silva. If the biggest importer in the world stops to import, this will affect the rest; if it goes out ready to face competition, this will affect all other producers.

The big banks from the developed countries emulate and try to establish coordinations with the banks of the

United States. If the US banks go into bankruptcy, the developed countries banks will go into bankruptcy too, and they will devour each other.

Fiscal heavens are thriving; peoples are suffering. Could humankind's well-being be guaranteed this way?

Bush's Self Criticism

SEPTEMBER 25, 2008

In a brief 15-minute speech, the President of the United States made some assertions that, had they come from the mouths of any of his adversaries, would have been described as atrocious and cynical slanders against the economic system of his country which he named "democratic capitalism."

After dramatically appealing to Congress to allocate an additional 700 billion dollars to cope with the crisis, he cited, among others, the following reasons:

· This is an extraordinary period for America's economy.

· We have seen terrible situations in the U.S. economy.

· The aim is to preserve the country's overall economy.

· I have declared that our global economy remains regulated largely by twentieth century laws and we must update it to the financial structure of the twenty-first century.

· Banks have restricted credits.

· Many lenders have approved loans without examining ability to pay.

· How did we reach this point? What does this mean for the country's financial future?

· Economists suggest these are problems that have developed for more than a decade.

· Most economists agree that the problems we're witnessing today developed over a long period of time.

· Many entrepreneurs got loans to start businesses, buy houses and cars. There were many negative consequences, particularly in the housing market.

· Many mortgage lenders approved loans for borrowers without carefully examining their ability to pay.

· Many people assumed they would be able to pay their mortgages, but it was not so.

· All this had effects far beyond the housing market.

· Securities are sold to investors around the world. Many assumed these securities had a tangible value.

· Many companies like Freddie Mac borrowed enormous sums of money and put our financial market at risk.

· The large banks found themselves saddled with large amounts of assets they could not sell.

· Other banks found themselves in similar situations and available credit dried up.

· Many believed they were guaranteed by the federal government and put our financial system at risk.

· The situation became more precarious by the day.

· I'm a strong believer in free enterprise.

· The decline in the housing market set off a domino effect.

· I believe companies that make bad decisions should pay for it. Under normal circumstances, I would have not followed this course. But these are not normal circumstances.

· The market is not functioning properly. There has been a widespread loss of confidence.

· The government's top economic experts warn that, without immediate action, the country could slip into panic, more banks could fail, there would be negative effects on the retirement accounts, foreclosures would rise and millions of Americans could lose their jobs.

· The country could experience a long and painful recession. We must not let this happen.

· Many are asking, how would a rescue plan work?

· It should be enacted as soon as possible.

· The federal government would put up to $700 billion to inject liquidity.

· The government will try to have the markets back to normal as soon as possible.

· We have seen how one company can grow so large that its failure jeopardizes the entire financial system.

· The government should be authorized to take a closer look at the companies to ensure that their growth does not threaten the global economy.

· Democratic capitalism is the best system ever devised.

· I know that Americans sometimes get discouraged, but this is a temporary situation.

· History has shown that, in times of real trial, its leaders unite to rise to the occasion.

· Tomorrow, in the White House, Obama, McCain and other congressional leaders will meet.

He concluded with thanks.

Some have pointed out that his eyes did not for one

minute move away from the teleprompter and that he was frowning.

Yesterday, George W. Bush did not only confess these truths; he launched a new sort of Alliance for Progress.

The first of them all was the colossal farce at Punta del Este in 1961, conceived by Kennedy after the Cuban Revolution.

The one before the last, as we know, was Bill Clinton's and it was called the Free Trade Area for the Americas (FTAA), which was signed in 1994. This one received its *coup de grâce* in Mar del Plata in the year 2005.

On the same day of his "self-criticism," Bush launched the Pathways to Prosperity in the Americas Initiative. What a ridiculous name.

After checking the list of the ten Latin American countries committed to the Initiative in New York, I realized the absence of Brazil, Argentina, Uruguay, Paraguay, Bolivia, Ecuador, Venezuela and Nicaragua; in other words, almost all of South America and one from Central America, whose former Chancellor, Miguel D'Escoto, a Sandinista and a priest who favour the Theology of Liberation, is now presiding over the United Nations General Assembly.

According to Bush's recurring fantasy, this project which is being discussed by the news cable agencies, as expressed by the President when he addressed the governments of the ten countries present, "would permit us to work to ensure that the benefits of trade are broadly shared."

"It will deepen the connections among regional markets. It will expand our cooperation on development issues."

"It is a good idea to continue opening up new markets, especially in our own neighbourhood."

Such events constitute excellent study material for the ideological battle.

What kind of progress can imperialism guarantee for any Latin American country, with its atomic weapons, its arms industry, its escorted fleets of nuclear aircraft carriers, its wars of conquest, its unequal exchange and permanent pillaging of other peoples?

Self-criticism is not a category under "democratic capitalism." Anyway, we shouldn't be ungrateful or impolite: we should thank Bush for his brilliant contribution to political theory.

The Law of the Jungle

Trade, within a society and between countries, is the exchange of goods and services produced by human beings. The owners of the means of production appropriate the profits. As a class, they are the leaders of the capitalist state and they boast of fostering development and social wellbeing through market. This they worship as an infallible God.

In every country there is competition between the strongest and the weakest; the ones with more physical energy and better fed, those who learned how to read and write, who attended school and have more experience accumulated; the ones with more extensive social relations and more resources, and those within society who fail to have these advantages.

Now, as far as the countries are concerned, there are differences between those with a better climate and more arable land, more water and more natural resources in the area where they are located, when there are no more territories to conquer; the ones mastering technology, having greater development and handling unlimited media resources and those who, on the contrary, do not enjoy any of these prerogatives. These are the sometimes enormous differences between the rich and the poor nations.

It's the law of the jungle.

There are no differences between ethnic groups, however, when it comes to the mental faculties of the human being. This has been thoroughly proven by science. The present society is not the natural way in which human life evolved, but rather a creation of the mentally developed man without which his life would be inconceivable. Therefore, what is at stake is whether the human being will be able to survive the privilege of having a creative mind.

The developed capitalist system, epitomized by the country with a privileged nature where the European white man brought his ideas, dreams and ambitions, is today in a crisis. But, it is not the usual crisis happening once in a number of years; not even the traumatic crisis of the 1930s but the worst of all crises since the world started to pursue this growth and development model.

The current crisis of the developed capitalist system is taking place when the empire is about to change leadership in the elections to be held in twenty-five days; it was all that was left to see.

The candidate of the two main parties that will say the last word in these elections are trying to persuade the bewildered voters — many of whom have never cared to cast a vote — that as candidates to the presidency they can secure the wellbeing and consumerism of what they describe as a people of middle class only, even though they are not planning to introduce any real changes to what they consider the most perfect economic system the world has ever known. The same world that, in their respective minds, is less important than the happiness of over three hundred million people who account for less than five percent of the world population. The fate of the remaining ninety-five per cent of human beings, peace and war, the fit or unfit-for-breathing air, will highly depend on the decisions of the administrative leader of the empire, whether or not that constitutional position has any power at a time of nuclear weapons and space shields moved by computers in circumstances where every second counts and when ethical principles keep loosing their value. Still, the more or less nefarious role of the President of that country cannot be overlooked.

Racism is deeply-rooted in the United States where the mind of millions of people can hardly reconcile with the notion that a black man, with his wife and children could live in the White House, which is precisely called *White.*

It's a miracle that the Democratic candidate has not met the same destiny as Martin Luther King, Malcolm X and others who only a few decades ago dreamed of justice and equality. He is in the habit of looking at his adversary with serenity and of smiling at the dialectic predicament of an opponent gazing into space.

The Republican candidate, on the other hand, who likes to enhance his reputation as a belligerent man, was one of the worst students in his class at West Point. He has confessed that he did not know any Mathematics; it can thus be assumed that he knew less of the complicated economic science.

The truth is his adversary surpasses him in cleverness and composure.

Something McCain has aplenty is age, and his health condition is not safe.

I am bringing up these data to indicate that eventually — if anything went wrong with the candidate's health, in case he is elected — the lady of the rifle, the inexperienced former governor of Alaska could become President of the United States. It can be noticed that she does not know a thing.

Meditating on the current US public debt — $10,266 trillions — that President Bush is laying on the shoulders of the new generations in that country, I took to calculating how long it would take a man to count the debt that he has doubled in eight years.

A man working eight hours a day, without missing a second, and counting one hundred one-dollar bills per minute, during 300 days in the year, would need 710 billion years to count that amount of money.

I could not find a more graphic way to describe the volume of money that is practically mentioned every day now.

In order to avoid a general state of panic, the U.S. administration has declared that it will secure deposits that do not exceed 250 thousand dollars. It will be managing banks and such funds as Lenin would never have thought of counting with an abacus.

We might be wondering about the contribution of Bush's administration to Socialism. But, let's not entertain any illusions. Once the banking operations go back to normal, the imperialists will return the banks to the private business as some other countries in this hemisphere have already done. The people always foot the bill.

Capitalism tends to reproduce itself under any social system because it is based on selfishness and on man's instincts.

The only choice left to human society is to overcome this contradiction; otherwise it would not be able to survive.

At this time, the ocean of money being poured into the world finances by the central banks of the developed capitalist countries is dealing a hard blow to the Stock Exchanges of the countries which resort to these institutions in an effort to beat their economic underdevelopment. Cuba has no Stock Exchange. We shall certainly find more rational and more socialist ways of financing our development.

The current crisis and the brutal measures of the U.S. administration to save itself will bring more inflation, more devaluation of the national currencies, more painful losses in the markets, lower prices for basic export commodities and more unequal exchange. But, they will also bring to the peoples a better understanding of the truth, a greater conscience, more rebelliousness and more revolutions.

We shall see how the crisis develops and what happens in the United States in twenty-five days.

The White House Ghost

Three days ago, on Friday October 10, the world was shocked by the impact of the Wall Street financial crisis. There is no way to count the millions of dollars in paper money injected by the Federal Reserve into the world finances to keep up banking operations and to prevent savers from loosing their money.

The G-7 Finance ministers meeting has agreed to implement the following measures:

· "Take decisive measures and use every available instrument to back financial institutions of importance to the system and prevent their bankruptcy.
· "Take all the necessary steps to unfreeze the credit and monetary markets and to ensure that banks and other financial institutions have plenty of access to liquidity and funds.
· "To ensure that the banks and other major financial intermediaries, depending on their needs, can raise capital from both public and private sources in sufficient amounts to restore confidence and to enable them to make loans to families and businesses.
· "To ensure that the respective national insurance of deposits and guarantee schemes are robust and consistent so that the minor depositors continue to have confidence in the safety of their deposits.

· "To act, when appropriate, to re-launch the secondary markets for mortgages.

That same day, the U.S. Treasure Secretary confirmed that the government will purchase bank shares, thus joining the British initiative. Both the United States and Great Britain have indicated that they will purchase preferential shares which are the first to report dividends but have no right to vote.

President Bush deemed his presence unnecessary at that meeting of finance ministers. He will meet with them on Saturday. Where was he on Friday October 10? No less than in Miami. He was attending a fundraising for Florida Republican candidates. Actually, with a 24 per cent approval rate he is the head of State with the least support in the entire history of the United States. He was meeting with business people and ringleaders of the Cuban scum in Miami. There he was, driven by his maniac anti-Cuban obsession, at the end of his gloomy two terms as leader of the empire. He could not even count on the support of the Cuban-American National Foundation set up by Reagan as part of his crusade against Cuba.

For purely demagogical reasons, that organization had publicly asked him to provisionally lift the ban on sending direct assistance to relatives and others affected by the devastating hurricanes which hit our people. Raul Martinez, a former mayor of Hialeah and a rival of Congressman Lincoln Diaz-Balart, had criticized the current policy of the man who was elected President by fraudulent means with less national votes than his adversary, due to Florida's weight in the electoral vote count, when he failed to have a majority even there.

On Sunday October 12, the European Union chaired by France agreed to request from the United States the organization of a summit conference to "reestablish the international financial system." This much was stated by President Sarkozy after a meeting in Paris of the euro zone countries.

Sarkozy indicated that Europe should now join the United States and other powers to go to the source of the financial crisis which has sunk the stock markets.

"We should persuade our American friends of the need for an international summit to reestablish the financial system," said Sarkozy, current President of the EU. It will not be a gift to the banks, the French President emphasized.

The President of the United States, George Bush, enters today his last 100 days in power overshadowed by very high unpopularity rates and one of the worst economic crises in recent decades.

On the other hand, Brazilian minister of Treasure Guido Mantega criticized the IMF today for describing the advanced nations as models to pursue. He also said that the standards of these nations should not prevail in the future reform of the financial system.

"The world is watching in awe how the present crisis exposes serious policy weaknesses and mistakes of countries that were considered models and offered as reference of good governance," said Mantega at the International Monetary and Financial Committee, the leading organ of the IMF.

With an economy torn to pieces, the United States

President, who reached that position in such an irregular and irresponsible way, has put in a real predicament all of its NATO allies and Japan, the U.S.' most developed and the wealthiest military, economic and technological partner in the Pacific.

Miami is today a madhouse and Bush has turned into a ghost.

The Stock Exchanges could not fall lower because they were already on the floor. Today, they were breathing happily thanks to the enormous injections of money artificially inflating them at the expense of the future. However, this absurdity cannot last. Bretton Woods is crumbling. The world will never be the same.

It's Amazing

Following an initiative from Sarkozy, President of France, on Sunday October 12th, the countries of the Euro zone agreed on an anti-crisis scheme.

On Monday 13th, an announcement is made that the European countries will inject multimillion amounts of money in the financial market to prevent a collapse. The stocks have risen after the amazing news.

Based on the abovementioned agreement, Germany had committed 480 billion Euros to the bailout operation; France, 360 billion; Holland, 200 billion; Austria and Spain, 100 billion each, and so on until with Great Britain's contribution they reached the figure of 1.7 trillion Euros. On that day — since the exchange rate between currencies constantly varies — that figure equaled 2.2 trillion U.S. dollars, which added to the 700 billion dollars allocated by the United States.

The shares of the major corporations, which were not bankrupt, witnessed a steep climbing of their value. This was far from compensating the losses sustained in the nine tragic days but it will give bankers and politicians from the capitalist developed world some breathing space.

In the evening of that same day, during a banquet in his honour offered at the White House, Prime Minister of Italy Silvio Berlusconi makes a speech paying homage to Bush: "We have confidence in the President who had the courage to do what he considered fair, what he had to do for himself, for his people and for the world."

He really went too far!

Also on the 13th, United States citizen Paul Krugman was presented with the 2008 Nobel Prize of Economics. He is certainly an advocate of the capitalist system but he is at the same time very critical of President Bush.

On the 14th, *El Pais* runs an article under the heading *Gordon has done it right* with some ideas that deserve to be literally reproduced:

"It's only natural that to face the need for financial capital the State provides the financial institutions with more capital in exchange for part of their properties . . .

"This kind of temporary and partial nationalization was also the solution privately favoured by Ben Bernanke, chairman of the Federal Reserve.

"On announcing his financial assistance scheme of 500 billion Euros, Henry Paulson, U.S. Treasure Secretary, was rejecting this obvious solution arguing that 'this is what you do in case of bankruptcy'.

"The British government has gone straight to the source of the problem and acted with incredible speed to solve it.

"After supposedly wasting several precious weeks, Paulson has also backpedaled. Now, he intends to buy bank shares instead of toxic mortgage assets.

"As I have said, we still don't know if these measures will work . . . That clear vision had to come from London and not from Washington.

"It's difficult to avoid feeling that Paulson's initial response was distorted by ideology. Remember that he is working for a government whose philosophy can be summed up in this phrase: 'what's private is good, what's public is bad'.

"In the executive all the expert professionals have been removed from office. Perhaps, there is no one in the Treasury now with the necessary history and stature to say to Paulson that what he was doing made no sense.

"Fortunately for the world economies what Gordon Brown and his ministers are doing do make sense. Perhaps, they have showed us the way out of this crisis."

As the 2008 Nobel Prize of Economics has confessed, he is not even sure himself that these measures will work.

This is really amazing.

On Tuesday 14th, the shares in the Stock Exchange lost a few points. The smiles were more stereotyped.

The European capitalist countries, saturated of productive capacity and commodities, are desperately in need of markets to avoid blue-collar and services workers lay-offs, to prevent savers from loosing their money and peasants from going broke. They are in no position to impose conditions and solutions to the rest of the world. That much has been proclaimed by important leaders from emerging countries and from those that being poor and economically plundered are the victims of unequal exchange.

Today, Wednesday 15th, the value of the shares in the Stock Market fell again with a loud crash.

Tonight, McCain and Obama will be passionately arguing the economic issue.

In the great U.S. democracy, half of those eligible to vote are not registered, and half of those who are registered do not vote. Thus, the rulers are elected by only 25 per cent of the electorate. Many of those who would perhaps like to vote for the African American candidate cannot do it.

According to the polls, that candidate has an overwhelming majority. However, no one dares say what might be the outcome.

The great economic crisis affecting the American society makes November 4 a day of paramount interest to the world public opinion.

In terms of elections, only one thing is certain: in the next British elections Gordon Brown will not be elected Primer Minister.

Economic Illiteracy

OCTOBER 26, 2008

In Zulia, Chavez made reference to "comrade Sarkozy." This remark carried some irony but he meant no offense. On the contrary, he was rather recognizing the sincerity of the President when he spoke in Beijing in his capacity as chairman of the European Community.

Nobody was saying what every European leader knows but would rather avoid: that the current financial system is useless and must be changed. The Venezuelan President candidly proclaimed:

"It is not possible to re-found the capitalist system; it would be like trying to sail on the Titanic when it's laying on the ocean floor."

According to press dispatches, at the meeting of the European and Asian Nations Association attended by 43 countries, Sarkozy made remarkable confessions:

"The situation is not good for the world which is facing an unprecedented financial crisis marked by its magnitude, swiftness and violence, a crisis whose consequences on the environment call into question the survival of mankind, as 900 million people lack the means to feed themselves.

"The countries taking part in this meeting account for two thirds of the global population and half its wealth. The financial crisis started in the United States, but it is now a global crisis demanding a global response.

"An eleven-year-old boy's place is not in a factory but in a school.

"No region in the world has a lesson to teach others." This is a clear reference to the United States.

Finally, he recalled before the Asian nations the colonial past of Europe in that continent.

If *Granma* had written such words, they would have been considered a cliché of the official communist press.

German Chancellor Angela Merkel said in Beijing that it was not possible "to foresee the magnitude and duration of the current international financial crisis. We are actually dealing with the inception of a new constituent Charter of finances." That same day the news revealed the general uncertainty unleashed.

The 43 countries from Europe and Asia gathering in Beijing agreed that the IMF should play a major role in assisting the countries most seriously afflicted by the crisis. They also supported an interregional summit to promote stability in the long run and the development of the world economy.

The President of the Spanish government, Rodriguez Zapatero, stated that "there is a crisis of responsibility which has enabled a few to grow richer while the majority is increasingly poor." He also said that "the markets have lost confidence in the market," and he urged the countries to fend off protectionism as he is convinced that competition will force the financial markets to play their role. He has not been officially invited to the Washington summit since Bush resents his withdrawing of the Spanish troops from Iraq.

The European Community President, Jose Manuel

Durao Barroso, upheld his warning on protectionism.

The UN Secretary General, Ban Ki-Moon, had his own meeting with outstanding economists trying to prevent that the developing countries become the main victims of the crisis.

The former Foreign Minister of the Sandinista Revolution and current President of the UN General Assembly, Miguel D'Escoto, asked that the issue of the financial crisis be not discussed among the wealthiest nations and a group of emerging countries that make up the G-20 but rather at the United Nations.

There are discrepancies about the venue and the meeting where a new financial system should be adopted that would put an end to chaos and to the absolute lack of security for the peoples. There is much fear that the wealthiest countries in the world, meeting with a small group of emerging nations enduring the financial crisis, might end up adopting a new Bretton Woods in disregard of the rest of the world. President Bush said yesterday that "the countries that will discuss here next month the global crisis should also renew their commitment to the basics of economic growth on a long term basis: free markets, free enterprise and free trade."

The banks were lending tens of dollars for every dollar deposited by the savers. They multiplied the money. They breathed and perspired through every pore. Any contraction led to ruin or to absorption by other banks. They had to be saved; always at the expense of the taxpayers. They were amassing great fortunes. Their privileged majority shareholders could afford to pay any money for anything.

Shi Jianxun, a professor at the Tongui University in Shanghai, claimed in an article he published in the foreign edition of *The People's Daily* that "the harsh reality has made the people realize, amidst the panic, that the United States has used the predominance of the dollar to plunder the riches of the world. There is a pressing need to change the international monetary system based on the predominant position of the dollar."

He used few words to explain the essential role of currencies in the international economic relations. This had been happening for centuries between Asia and Europe. Let's not forget that opium was imposed on China as a currency. I already addressed this when I wrote "The Chinese Victory."

The authorities of that country would not even receive the metal silver initially used by the Spaniards from their colony in the Filipinas to pay for the products purchased in China, because it was progressively devaluated due to the abundance of this metal in the New World recently conquered by Europe. Today, the European leaders feel embarrassed by the things they had imposed on China for centuries.

According to the Chinese economist, the existing difficulties with the terms of trade between these two continents should be resolved with euros, pound sterling, yens and yuans. Undoubtedly, a reasonable regulation between these four currencies would help in the development of fair trade relations between Europe, Great Britain, Japan and China.

Two countries which produce sophisticated equipment with state-of-the-art technology, both for production and services, such as Japan and Germany would be included in that area, as well as the potentially largest engine pushing the world economy, China, with a close to 1.4 billion population and over $1.5 trillion in its hard currency reserves mostly in U.S. dollars and Treasury bonds. Japan is only second with almost an identical amount of hard currency reserves.

At the present juncture, the value of the dollar is increased by this currency's predominant position imposed on the world economy as the Shanghai professor has rightly indicated and rejected.

A large number of Third World countries, which are exporters of goods and raw materials with little added value, are importers of Chinese consumer goods. These usually have reasonable prices, unlike Japanese and German goods which tend to be increasingly expensive. Even when China has tried to prevent the overvaluation of the yuan, as the Yankees have constantly demanded to protect their industries from Chinese competition, the value of the yuan increases and the purchasing power of our exports decreases.

The price of nickel, our main export item, whose value recently was over 50,000 dollars, now hardly reaches 8,500 dollars a ton, that is, less than 20 per cent of the top price it had enjoyed. The price of copper has decreased to less than 50 per cent, and the same is true of iron, aluminum, tin, zinc, and every other mineral indispensable for a sustained development. And defying any rational or common sense, the price of consumer goods such as coffee, cocoa, sugar and others has barely grown in over 40 years. This is the reason why not long ago I also warned that as a result of an impending crisis, the markets would be lost and the purchasing power of our products would be considerably reduced. The developed capitalist nations are well aware that under such circumstances their factories and services would be paralyzed, and only the consumption capacity of a large part of mankind already living at the poverty line or under this level, would keep them going.

This is the great dilemma raised by the financial crisis and the danger that social and national selfishness will prevail regardless of the wishes of many politicians and statesmen agonizing over this phenomenon. They have no confidence in the system from which they emerged as public men.

After the people have left illiteracy behind; when they have learned how to read and write and they have an indispensable minimum knowledge allowing them to live and produce honestly, they still need to overcome the worst form of ignorance in our times: economic illiteracy. It's the only way to know what's happening in the world.

The Worst Choice

OCTOBER 30, 2008

Today, I read that the U.S. Federal Reserve had opened a new line of credit for the Central Banks of Mexico, Brazil, South Korea and Singapore.

The same report claimed that similar credits have been issued to the Central Banks of Australia, Canada, Denmark, the United Kingdom, Japan, New Zealand, Switzerland and the European Central Bank.

Based on these agreements, the Central Banks shall receive funds in exchange for hard currency reserves from these countries which have sustained considerable losses due to the trade and financial crisis.

This way the economic power of the US currency is asserted, a privilege granted at Bretton Woods.

The International Monetary Fund, which is the same people under a different name, has announced the release of high sums of money to its clients in Eastern Europe. Hungary will be receiving the equivalent of $20 billion euros; a large part of these are dollars coming from the United States. The machines keep minting bills and the IMF keeps granting its unfair loans.

On the other hand, the World Wild Fund stated in Geneva yesterday that at the present spending rate, by 2030 humanity will need the resources of two planets to keep up its life style.

The WWF is a serious institution. There is no need to be a University graduate of Mathematics, Economics or

Political Sciences to understand what this means. It's the worst choice. The developed capitalism hopes to continue plundering the world as if the world could still stand it.

Meeting Lula

It's not the money injection *per se* to the developing countries that I criticized in my reflection yesterday, as some press dispatches chose to interpret.

When I spoke of *the worst choice*, I was thinking of the objectives of the money injection and the way it was given. I have been analyzing the idea that the financial crisis is the consequence of the privileges granted to the United States developed capitalism at Bretton Woods in 1944. At the end of World War II, this country was emerging with a considerable economic and military power. The phenomenon tends to repeat itself every so often.

Upon President of Brazil Lula da Silva's arrival in the country, I addressed him a letter. We had not scheduled a meeting during his short visit to our country. On the abovementioned point I wrote:

"Whoever becomes the United States leader after the current crisis should feel a rising pressure from all of the Third World countries towards solutions involving every nation and not only a few of them. The wealthiest nations are in desperate need of the poor nations' consumption, otherwise their goods and services production centres would be paralyzed. Let them use their computers to estimate how many trillions they'll need to invest to enable the poor nations to develop while preventing the destruction of the environment and life on our planet."

Any reader can see that when I speak of investing in the Third World, I mean making a contribution in funds, basically as soft loans, with almost no interest, in order to promote a rational ecology-friendly development.

I could meet with Lula who asked to see me despite his tight schedule. We talked for almost two hours. I explained to him that I would be making public the concepts contained in my letter. He did not raise any objection. Our conversation was, as usual, pleasant and respectful. He related to me in detail the work he is carrying out in his country. I thanked him for Brazil's political and economic support to Cuba in its struggle and emphasized the decisive role played by Venezuela, a Latin American developing country and its President, in the most critical days of the Special Period and today, as the imperialist blockade has tightened and our country has just endured the scourge of two devastating hurricanes.

Despite our broad exchange, he was free an hour and a half before the time scheduled for his departure.

As I could see in the press reports this afternoon, he adopted a brave position with regards to the United States elections. If McCain were elected, he would not be able to count beforehand with the largest Latin American country: Brazil.

The G-20 meeting convened by Bush will be held in Washington next November 15. The first thing you see as you turn on a TV set is a Head of State addressing a high level gathering. I wonder how much time is left to the Heads of State to be informed about and to meditate on the complex problems afflicting the world.

The current President of the United States has no problem at all. He does not solve problems, he creates them.

Much Ado About Nothing

NOVEMBER 16, 2008

Bush seemed happy to have Lula seated on his right during dinner on Friday. Hu Jintao, whom he respects for his country's enormous market, the capacity to produce consumer goods at low cost and the volume of his reserves in U.S. dollars and bonds, was seated to his left.

Medvedev, whom he has offended with the threat of locating strategic radars and missiles not far from Moscow, was assigned a seat at a distance from the White House host.

The king of Saudi Arabia, a country that, in the near future, will be producing 15 million tons of light oil at highly competitive prices, was also sitting on his left, beside Hu.

Meanwhile, his most loyal ally in Europe, British Prime Minister Gordon Brown, could not be seen close to him in the footage.

Nicolas Sarkozy, who is not happy with the present architecture of the financial order, was at a distance from him, with a pained expression on his face.

In the television coverage of the meal, I couldn't even see the president of the Spanish Government, José Luis Rodríguez Zapatero, a victim of Bush's personal resentment and also present at the Washington conclave.

That is how those attending the banquet were seated.

Anyone would have assumed that the following day there would be a profound debate on the thorny issue.

Early Saturday morning, the press agencies were reporting on the programme that would unfold at the National Building Museum in Washington, D.C. Every second was covered. There would be an analysis of the current crisis and the measures to be taken. It would start at 11:30 a.m. local time. First, there would be a photo op, or "family picture," as Bush called it, and 20 minutes later the first plenary session would start followed by a another one in the second half of the day. Everything was strictly planned, even the majestic sanitary services.

The speeches and analysis would last approximately three hours and 30 minutes. At 3:25 local time, lunch, immediately followed by the final declaration at 5:05. One hour later, at 6:05, Bush would leave to relax, have dinner and sleep placidly in Camp David.

The day passed by, for those following the event, with an impatience to know how the problems of the planet and the human species could be dealt with in such a short space of time. A final declaration had been announced.

The fact is that the final declaration of the Summit was drafted by pre-selected economic advisors, very close to neoliberal thinking while, in pre- and post-Summit statements, Bush demanded more power and more money for the International Monetary Fund, the World Bank and other world institutions under the rigorous control of the United States and its closest allies. That country had decided to inject $700 billion to bail out its banks and multinational corporations. Europe offered a similar or higher figure. Japan, its strongest pillar in Asia, has promised a contribution of $100 billion. In the case of the People's Republic of China, which is developing increasing and advisable relations with Latin American countries, it is expected to make a further contribution of $100 billion dollars from its reserves.

Where could so many dollars, euros and pounds sterling come from, as if they are not seriously indebting new generations? How can the structure of the new world economy be built on paper money, which is what is really being put into circulation immediately, when the country issuing it is suffering from an enormous fiscal deficit? Is so much air travel to a point on the planet called Washington to meet with a President with only 60 more days left in government to sign a document previously designed to be adopted at the Washington Museum? Was the U.S. radio, TV and press right in not paying special attention to this old imperialist replay in the much-trumpeted meeting?

What is really incredible is the final declaration adopted by consensus in the conclave. It is obvious that it constitutes a full acceptance of Bush's demands before and during the Summit. A number of the participating countries had no choice but to adopt it; in their desperate struggle for development, they do not want to be isolated from the richest and most powerful and their financial institutions, which constitute a majority in the G-20.

Bush spoke with veritable euphoria, using demagogic phrases that mirror the final declaration.

He said: "The first decision I had to make was who was coming to the meeting. And obviously I decided that we ought to have the G-20 nations, instead of just the G-8 or the G-13. But once you make the decision to have the G-20, then the fundamental question is, with that many nations from six different continents, who all represent different stages of economic development, how is it possible to reach agreements that are substantial, and I'm pleased to report the answer to that question is that we have done so."

"The United States has taken some extraordinary measures. Those of you who have followed my career know that I'm a free market person — until you are told that if you don't take decisive measures then it's conceivable that our country could go into a depression greater than the Great Depression.

"[. . .] we just started on the $700 billion fund to start getting money out to our banks.

"[. . .] we all understand the need to work on pro-growth economic policies."

"Transparency is very important so that investors and regulators are able to know the truth."

The rest of what Bush said continues more or less along these lines.

The final declaration of the summit, which takes half an hour to read in public due to its length, clearly defines itself in a number of selected paragraphs:

"We, the leaders of the G-20 have held a first meeting in Washington, on November 15, in the light of serious challenges to the world economy and financial markets . . .

"[. . .] we should lay the foundations for a reform that will make this global crisis less likely to happen again in the future. Our work should be guided by the principles of the free market, free trade and investment . . ."

"[. . .] the market players sought to obtain higher

profits without making an adequate assessment of the risks and they failed . . ."

"The authorities, regulators and supervisors from some developed nations did not realize or were not adequately warned about the risks created in the financial markets . . ."

". . . insufficient and poorly coordinated macroeconomic policies as well as inadequate structure reforms, led to an unsustainable macroeconomic global result."

"Many emerging economies, that have helped sustain the world economy, are increasingly suffering the impact of world braking."

"We note the important role of the IMF in response to the crisis; we salute the new short-term liquidity mechanism and urge a constant review of its instruments to ensure flexibility."

"We shall encourage the World Bank and other multilateral developing banks to use their full capacity in support of their agenda for assistance . . ."

"We will ensure that the IMF, the World Bank and other multilateral developing banks have the necessary resources to continue playing their role in the solution of the crisis."

"We shall exercise a strong monitoring of the credit agencies through the development of an international code of conduct."

"We pledge to protect the integrity of the world financial markets by reinforcing protection to investors and consumers."

"We are committed to advance in the reform of the institutions of Bretton Woods so that they reflect the changes in the world economy in order to increase their legitimacy and effectiveness."

"We shall meet again on April 30, 2009, to review the implementation of the principles and decisions made today."

"We concede that these reforms will only be successful if they are based on a serious commitment to free market principles, including the rule of law, respect for private property, free trade and investment, efficient and competitive markets and effectively regulated financial systems."

"We shall refrain from erecting new barriers to investment and trade in goods and services."

"We are aware of the impact of the current crisis on the developing nations, especially on the most vulnerable."

"We are certain that as we advance through cooperation, collaboration and multilateralism we will overcome the challenges and restore stability and prosperity to the world economy."

Technocratic language, inaccessible to the masses.

Respect for the empire, whose abusive methods are not criticized in any way.

Praise for the IMF, the World Bank and the multilateral credit organizations, the engenders of debt, fabulous bureaucratic costs and investments directed at supplying raw materials to the large multinationals, which are also responsible for the crisis.

It goes on like that until the last paragraph. It is

boring, full of the usual rhetoric. It says absolutely nothing. It was signed by Bush, the champion of neoliberalism, the man responsible for massacres and genocidal wars, who has invested in his bloody adventures all the money that would have sufficed to change the economic face of the world.

The document does not say one word on the absurdity of the policy promoted by the United States to convert food into fuel; on the unequal exchange to which we, the nations of the Third World are subjected; or on the sterile arms race, the production and trade of weapons; the rupture of the ecological balance and the extremely serious threats to peace that are taking the world to the brink of annihilation.

Only one short four-word phrase lost in the lengthy document mentions the need "to face up to climate change."

One can see in the declaration how the countries attending the conclave are demanding to meet again in April 2009, in the United Kingdom, Japan or any other country that meets the necessary requirements — nobody knows which one — to examine the situation of the world finances, cherishing the dream that the cyclical crises with their dramatic consequences will never happen again.

Now is the time for the theoreticians from the left and the right to offer cool or heated opinions on the document.

From my point of view the privileges of the empire were not even touched upon. If one has the necessary patience to read it from the beginning to the end, it can be appreciated that it is simply a pious appeal to the ethic of the most powerful country on earth, both technologically and militarily, in the period of the globalization of the economy; rather like those who beg the wolf not to devour Little Red Riding Hood.

The Great Crisis of the 1930s

It is a difficult subject to explain, although it seems very simple. The U.S. Federal Reserve system was created in 1913 as the result of capitalism in full development. Salvador Allende, a man we all remember as from our era, had turned about 15 years old.

World War I broke out in 1914, when the heir prince to the Austrian-Hungarian Empire in the heart of central and southern Europe, was assassinated in Sarajevo. Canada was still a British colony. The GB pound sterling had the privilege of being the currency used internationally. The basic metal used to make it was gold, as it had been for more than 1,000 years in the capital of the Roman empire of the east, Constantinople. Those who began the bloody battles against Muslims in the Near East, brandishing religious pretexts, were feudal knights of the Christian kingdoms of Europe, whose real purpose was to control trade routes and other mundane, more vulgar goals that could be addressed on another occasion.

The United States began to participate in World War I toward the end, in 1917, two years after the sinking of the *Lusitania*, which was carrying U.S. passengers who had departed from New York. It was sunk by torpedoes fired from a German submarine with absurd instructions to attack a ship flying the flag of a distant, rich and potentially powerful country that, under the cover of supposed neutrality, intended to find a pretext to participate in the war on the side of Britain, France and their allies. The attack took place on May 7, 1915, as the ship was crossing the strait between Ireland and England. In the 20 minutes it took to founder, very few passengers were able to abandon ship; the 1,198 people who were still aboard perished.

The growth of the U.S. economy after that war was maintained continuously, except for cyclical crises that were resolved by the Federal Reserve system (FED), without more serious consequences.

On October 24, 1929, remembered in U.S. history as "Black Thursday," the economic crisis broke out. The Reserve Bank of New York, which is based on Wall Street, just like other banks and corporations — according to the right-wing theorist and renowned U.S. economist Milton Friedman, Nobel laureate in economics (1976), reacted "instinctively," adopting the measures that he considered to be most correct: "of putting money into circulation." The Reserve Bank in Washington, accustomed to the pre-eminence of its opinions, was able to finally impose the opposite idea. The secretary of the Treasury under President Hoover supported the Reserve Bank of Washington, and the one in New York ended up giving way. "But the worst was yet to come," stated Friedman, who explains more clearly than any other eminent economist — some of them from the opposite tendency — the sequence of events, when he wrote, "Until the fall of 1930, the recession in economic activity, despite being serious, was not affected by financial difficulties or the petitions of depositors who were trying to withdraw their deposits. The character of the recession changed drastically when a series of bankruptcies in the midwestern and southern United States weakened people's confidence in banks and resulted in numerous attempts to convert bank deposits into cash.

"On December 11, 1930, the Bank of the United States closed. It was the critical date. It was the largest commercial bank ever to collapse in U.S. history."

In the month of December 1930 alone, 352 banks closed their doors. "The FED could have reached a better solution by making a large-scale buyout on the market of public debt securities.

"In September 1931, the date on which Britain abandoned the gold standard, it followed a policy that was even more negative.

"The system reacted after two years of hard repression, increasing that type of interest to a level never reached in its history."

We should take into account that Friedman is reflecting an opinion that still predominates in official U.S. circles almost 80 years later.

"In 1932, the FED, under pressure from Congress, ended its period of sessions and immediately cancelled its buying programme.

"The final episode was the bank panic of 1933.

"Fear intensified during the interregnum between Herbert Hoover and Franklin D. Roosevelt, elected on November 8, 1932, but whose inauguration did not take place until March 4, 1933. The first did not wish to take any drastic measures without the cooperation of the new president, while Roosevelt, for his part, did not want to assume any responsibilities until he was sworn in."

The episode reminds us of what is happening today with the president elected in the recent November 4 elections, less than a month ago, Barack Obama, who will succeed Bush on January 20, 2009. Only the period of interregnum has changed; in the 1930s, it was no more than 117 days, and currently it is no more than 77.

Right during the peak of the economic boom, according to Friedman, there were as many as 25,000 banks in the United States. At the start of 1933, the number had gone down to 18,000.

"When President Roosevelt decided to end the bank closure, 10 days after it had begun," Friedman said, "something less than 12,000 banks were authorized to open their doors, to which only 3,000 were added later. Therefore, altogether, about 10,000 of the 25,000 banks existing in 1929 disappeared during those four years, via a process of bankruptcy, merger or liquidation.

"The closure of businesses, falling production and growing unemployment all fuelled nervousness and fear.

"Once the depression was underway, it spread to other countries and, of course, there was a reflexive influence; another example of the realignment so omnipresence in a complex economy," Friedman concludes.

The world of 1933 that he referred to in his book is nothing at all like today's, which is totally globalized, comprising more than 190 states represented at the UN, whose inhabitants are all being threatened by dangers that scientists — even the most optimistic — cannot ignore, and that a growing number of people know about and agree on, including prominent U.S. politicians.

The echo of the repercussion of the current crisis can

be seen in the desperate efforts of major world leaders.

The Xinhua agency reports that President Hu Jintao of the People's Republic of China, a country that has experienced sustained, two-digit growth in recent years, warned yesterday that "China is under growing pressure because of its enormous population, limited resources and environmental problems." It is the only country that we know has hard currency reserves of almost $2 trillion. The Chinese president lists "a series of essential steps for protecting the fundamental interests of the population and protecting the environment in the strategy of industrialization and modernization of China." He said, finally, that "with the propagation of the financial crisis, world demand for products has been considerably reduced."

With these words from the leader of the most populated country on the planet, it is not necessary to add more arguments concerning the profundity of the current crisis.